A Lift-the-Flap Book

Baby Giraffe

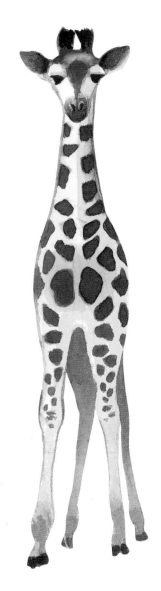

Adrienne Kennaway

Happy Cat Books

Text and illustrations copyright © Adrienne Kennaway, 1999

The moral right of the author/illustrator has been asserted

First published 1999 by Happy Cat Books, Bradfield, Essex CO11 2UT

A CIP catalogue record for this book is available from the British Library

ISBN 1 899248 18 8   Paperback
ISBN 1 899248 13 7   Hardback

Manufactured in China

Also illustrated by Adrienne Kennaway in Happy Cat Books

Baby Rhino's Escape
Bushbaby
Meerkat in Trouble

In the heart of Africa lived a family of giraffes…

One day Baby Giraffe was
munching leaves.
"Follow me," cried
a bird.

Suddenly Giraffe
heard running feet.

Then three other
animals rushed by.

Baby Giraffe galloped after them.

Ahead of him thundered mighty Elephant with two animals by his side.

"Quick, follow that bird!"

Soon they reached
the foot of a baobab
tree. From a hole in
the trunk came an
angry buzzing.

"Your stings don't hurt me, I've got thick fur," said Honey Badger as he scooped out honey.

As the animals ate the honeycomb, Baby Giraffe stretched out his tongue.

Baby Giraffe rushed to the river and dipped his
burning mouth in the cool water. That was better.

With a thundering of hooves a huge giraffe
burst into the clearing and charged Lion.

Baby Giraffe felt
so happy as he
rested close by his
mother's side.

"Best not to stray from
your herd," she said gently.